Oftentimes I Pause

Anna R. Davis

DEDICATION

For my grandpa who wrote great poetry of his own. I wish I could share these with him.

Anna R. Davis

CONTENTS

Oftentimes I Pause

ACKNOWLEDGMENTS

I am grateful to our family friend, Michael Leamy, who taught me about poetry and helped me put this book together.

Scripture taken from the New King James Version.

Introduction

It all started with rhyming words at two years of age. The sound these words made when put together intrigued me. Only years later, would I discover there was a lot more to poetry than that. Not until I was about twelve, did I start writing poetry and enjoying it. Poems were easier than stories; they had fewer words and didn't require complete sentences. I started letting friends read them. Their praise and encouragement is what brought success out of a very meager beginning. After reading some of my poetry, a good friend of our family offered to mentor me on the mechanics of poetry. (I had no idea what that meant at the time.) After a few months of explaining to me that poems had rules, that there were many different types of poetry, and that the poet had to choose his own scheme, he declared that I had "graduated from student to peer." I started becoming more flexible with my writing as I learned so many fun options. I did things that I once thought for me as unseemly, like writing a poem that did not rhyme. Soon poems started piling up. I had opportunities to share my poetry with groups of people such as when the Rescue Mission in our city held a talent show, at camp, and when I had a poem published in our community college magazine.

My dad has had a great influence on my writing life. Often I would let him read my poetry and seek his opinion. He just loved to read them. Several ideas threaded throughout my poems were influenced by him. He kept telling me "you've got to get your poems put together in a book." *So I did.*

ALWAYS PUT GOD FIRST

Our family and friends,
This life we hold so dear;
And someday might we have to part
With these we often fear.

The pastimes we enjoy,
A goal we reach with pride,
May take the place our Lord should be
And set His time aside.

Important things to us,
Should never take away
The precious moments we should spend
In prayer with God each day.

For truth might we pursue,
And for the Scriptures thirst;
So may we live this life on earth
To always put God first.

Garter Snake

A flash,
a molted skin
is often all we see of him;
A sudden move
in the grass
leaves a startled little lass.
His slender
body fits through
places accessed by so few.
An eager hunter
might prevail
to glimpse his striped retreating tail.
If he stops
for a rest,
perhaps he'll meet a grabby guest.
But though a hand
around him be,
he squirms and slips to liberty.
Walking through
the woods by day,
a rustle gives his spot away.
With no feet
he slithers on;
one looks, but he's already gone.

WHAT LOVE DOES NOT

In love there is no greed,
There is no cause for war;
To selfish things it won't take heed,
And love does not keep score.
With right does not dispute,
Love never will complain;
And truthfulness does not refute,
From good does not refrain.
And love will never hate,
It won't ignore command;
And does not ever hesitate
To lend a helping hand.
It never says "I can't,"
Or leaves behind its work;
And will not yield a fruitless plant;
Its duty does not shirk.
Its father won't defy,
Its mother will not grieve.
And it will never tell a lie,
For love does not deceive.
Hence, love will never cheat,
Or has conceited sought
For riches soon their end to meet.
All these things love does not.

I Could Stop

I could stop working,
But few producers live.
I could quit sharing
The blessings I've to give.
I could stop charging
A sweat to others help;
I could start waving
As dutiless as kelp.
Could simply chuck smiling,
For few such glow return.
'Twould easy be, needy
Men's service to adjourn.
I could stop praying
For enemies lost souls.
Soon instead of Jesus,
I've self let seize control.
I could stop writing,
And God-implanted words
In harmony's beauty,
Leave up to the birds.
But souls would be shrinking,
And God loves them all.
A traitor'd be thinking
To let weary fall.
My God formed a channel
From stubborn-born clay
To transmit His message
And point men His Way.

The Way We Are

A little stone
Sat all alone
Beneath the rippling stream,
And of his wish
To be a fish
He could but only dream,

And every day
With grief he'd say
As fish would pass him by,
Why can't I be
So fine like thee,
What poor a thing am I!

With wiggly tails,
And shiny scales
That gleam when touched by sun
You roam the sea,
So glad and free
With fins but I have none.

I sit alone,
Unseen, unknown
For no one thinks of me;
And what a prize
Are fishes eyes
But I have none to see.

And filled with woe
He failed to know
Whose presence slipped away
From certain death,
And caught its breath
Beneath the stone that day.

Yet unaware
Its life could spare
Inside the hidden cleft,
When safe again,
The tiny fin
And tail had swiftly left.

Oh, if the stone
Had only known
What purpose he partook!
That he was not
With error wrought,
Unseen below the brook.

So how much more
Has God in store
And planned for you and me?
Yet we complain
For selfish gain,
Indwelled with jealousy.

I wish I were
As fair as her,
Or maybe like the strong.
But did you not
Give second thought
That such a want is wrong?

And sulking there
In our despair,
God cares about us still.
Not knowing this,
We sadly miss
His good and perfect will.

For every man
He has a plan,
And for each woman too;
And though we're dust,
We still can trust
God's changing me and you.

So let us look
Into the brook,
And understand we may;
God didn't make
A sole mistake
When forming us this way.

That like the stone
We're not alone,
Although we feel afar,
For just is He
Who perfectly
Made us the way we are.

The Testing

Cross my frequent lane

One day

A knotted limb had craned,

Bidding of my hand

A fee to pay.

How do me so sass?

I frowned,

I'm always let to pass!

Whined the branch, don't yell,

The gust me downed.

So I grilled the wind

Why you?

You've always been my friend.

Came the swish reponse;

God sent me through.

Wild Whale

I dove into the sea.
The icy water
cringed at me.

Then down I sped, depths rose,
A different pressure
At my nose

Than at my fin and tail.
A fish school crossed my
Bubbly trail.

The darkness closed around
And light diminished
Without sound.

Reserving flicks of tail
To spray the boatsmen
At the sail.

An hour will pass, and I,
Without a warning.
Surface nigh,

Will break through, blocking sun,
Breathe, falling heavy;
Just for fun.

Someone

I saw the daisies bobbing
And a honeybee buzzing near,
And thought the feet of Someone
Had just been walking here.

I saw a spotted baby
Hop toward its mom, a deer,
And thought the eyes of Someone
Had just passed over here.

I saw the plunging water,
As the sunlit cascade did cheer,
And fancied Someone's presence
Was still left over here.

I saw the heaven night lights,
Each one was a sparkling gem,
And sensed the breath of Someone
Had just passed over them.

Chicks started their eggs pecking,
Their tiny chirps I could hear,
While thinking Someone else
Was then surely watching near.

I saw the rainbow colors
That sky with dark thunderclouds share,
And sensed the hand of Someone
Had just passed over there.

A butterfly was flitting,
How could he withstand the force
Of wind? And I guessed Someone
Was guiding him, of course.

I saw the mountains snowcapped,
Watched birds of all sorts in flight,
And thought just having made them
Was Someone's pure delight.

I saw an empty park bench,
And hoped my tired legs to spare,
It seemed the warmth of Someone
Had just been sitting there.

I floated on the river,
Attempted my boat to steer,
And felt the peace of Someone
Who'd just been over here.

I saw a salmon fighting
The current, but how'd he know
His homestream? I thought Someone
Had told him where to go.

The sunset was red glowing,
The clouds looked like horse's hair,
I knew the art of Someone
Had just been finished there.

I held a human baby ,
And on the sweet miracle smiled,
While being sure the Maker's arms
Also held this child.

As I am growing older,
I'm seeing life's hardships start,
I'm glad this special Someone
Is living in my heart.

"How You Will Know Them"

By looking at a person's boots,

You might know where they've been;

Examining a person's fruits

Will tell with whom they've been.

Matthew 7:20

THE WIND'S QUESTION

The wind asked me a question
To which I'd no reply:
What if God had sent you
To brush the wispy sky?

Would your molding crumble,
Being substance held
'Neath God's word or grumble;
Is such how man rebelled?

And you blessed with eternal
Possibilities and soul,
Gobble down the gifts unmindful
As birds do fishes whole.

You'd at his bid diminish
Like waves shore-sickened ebb,
Such simple call to finish
I'd rather spin a web?

Is God's work too undignified
For your prideful heart?
If you can't do a small job
Won't big ones fall apart?

Dancing Flamingoes on Sunset Waters

They flock, dusting from their wings
Drops of water with a shiver.
They lift one leg, balancing,
In the shallow rippled river.

They join, graceful, in ballet,
Gliding o'er the sun-sparked surface.
They leave a trail; colors stray
Like a star without a purpose

Or gold glistening through glass.
Heaven's contents lying shattered
Collect into a spangled mass.
By a touch again are scattered.

They fly, tracing stroke by stroke
The emotion of a Crafter.
And stir amidst twilight's cloak,
Wind-curled leaves in quiet laughter.

Against eve-hue's slow retreat,
Draws in dusk, the night ensnarer.
They etch a frame short to greet
Beauty in a natural mirror.

Around The River Bend

While pausing on my weary stroll,
A river bids me near
With curiosity as I
A voice begin to hear.

So very still and indistinct,
I barely catch the words
Above the water's surging rush
And chirping of the birds.

But once I'd stopped, the call was clear.
Be heedful, listen well;
Momentous is the parable
The river has to tell.

I saw a little drifting boat,
Its wooden oars were two,
And then I heard the whisper say
That vessel, child, is you.

The paddles held by Jesus Christ
Are not allowed to stray,
If you are willing to submit
And let Him guide the way.

The river runs to many forks
Where careful you must be,
For what's around the river bend,
The Lord alone can see.

And only the obedient,
His branch will truly know;
And won't abstain to follow it
Wherever it may go.

But life at times a current, lures
From God's protective keep,
Away from shallows mild and calm
Into the violent deep.

There storms await to sink your boat.
The jetting boulder's teeth
Desire to catch you in your fright
And drag you underneath.

But who is He who can upon
Its crashing surface stand,
And at your earnest, trusting plea,
Redeem you with His hand?

And bring you safely back again
Toward the shallows clear,
The oars within His grip once more,
Your worries disappear.

You've found the river's dangers lurk
In stretches far and wide,
And only with God's helping hand
You'll reach the other side.

At last you start to understand
And learn your closest friend
Is Jesus who alone can lead
Around the river bend.

Little Bird

You hop across the winter ground.
Your tiny feet are cold;
And though you have no berries found,
So vigilant and bold

You seek unfailingly and sing
Your sweet, unflustered tune.
Unconscious that no food will bring
You certain death, and soon.

But 'neath the morning frost, behold;
You spy them scattered there.
Without a minute to be lost
And not a seed to spare,

You quickly clean the ground of them
While whispering a prayer
Of thankfulness, and with your fill,
Your wings take to the air.

God Chose A Donkey

Come, children, listen to grandfather's talk,
Called mother donkey at seven o'clock.
Soon to have bedtime, the young ones would trot
Quickly to win for themselves the best spot.

Back in the warmth of the stable-strewn hay,
And after all silenced of whinny and bray,
Grandfather donkey's tradition would live;
He'd clear first his throat, a long reminisce give.

Yet none did it bore, for he captured the word.
He promised this story they never had heard.
I once was a young donkey, yes, even I,
That time when a kick louder speaks than a cry.

I spotted my chance to steer free of the plow,
Though plots with achievement time wouldn't allow.
So as you'd imagine I did not succeed;
A rope and a tree trunk were easy to read.

It wasn't much later, I, fixed in my place,
Resorted to stamping, the sun in my face,
Two men unfamiliar came loos'ning my reins.
For freedom the blood spurted wild in my veins.

Upon but that moment my owner caught sight,
And questioned their taking his animal right.
Their answer came sudden to change my intent;
Our Master has spoken, so with them I went.

All new the surroundings, my interest poured.
We stopped near a city and there was the Lord!
The first weight I'd ever to hold on my back
Cost Jesus no sternness, no labor, no whack.

I'm least of worthless that He'd chosen me,
The lowest of ridden, no comfort to be.
Yet lifted He was while I stood deadly still,
As people excited the streets came to fill.

They swayed in their hands and they threw to the ground;
A road paved with palm branches, Christ's entry crowned.
And even their garments some spread on the way.
I carried the King to the temple that day.

Now young ones, remember, this story is true.
Pass on to your children and their children too,
That time in Jerusalem God used an ass,
Unbroken, to bring Him where death soon would pass.

Now grandfather donkey for sleep bowed his head,
And by all his wisdom was followed to bed.
He'd dream of the moments he serviced his King,
The joyful hosanna's still heard people sing.

THE DEER

Dawn is breaking,
Leaves are shaking
In the frigid breeze;
Eagles
soaring,
Color
pouring
O'er the rising
trees.
And appearing

In the clearing,
Promptly gazing round;
Slowly
walking,
Both ears
cocking
For the slightest
sound.
Then rebounding,
Sure hooves pounding;
Vanishing from sight.
Ever running
From the cunning,
This its lifelong plight.

Once An Empty Seashell

'Twas down upon the beach one day,
I hoped to lucky be;
To find a trove of shells diverse,
Complete and fracture free.

For frequently I'd come to search,
My bucket soon would fill
With specimens unique and bright,
But it was empty still.

And now for hours, I'd strolled and searched,
While nothing had I found.
Dismayed and tired, I rested then
And listened to the sound

Of beating surf against the shore,
When seemingly a voice
Came forward from the ocean's mouth:
To harken is a choice.

But if you heed these honest words,
You might discover, child,
The creature God did love the most;
When Jesus saw and smiled.

The image formed in likeness of
The Maker, great I Am;
And given life with his own breath,
From Whom all good things stem.

Although He made the universe,
The boundless cosmos strew,
He cherishes all sinful men;
He loves and cares for you.

The gulls above, as well, agreed
That God gave man the right
To have dominion, and was deemed
Most precious in His sight.

The voices died, the sky ablaze.
My fingers turned the sand
While pond'ring all these things in mind;
I didn't understand.

Did God still care for micro me?
My worth seemed mighty small.
Did that same God who formed my soul,
Still love me after all?

When I discovered what a darkness
My own heart possessed.
How could He look upon my messed
Up life and not detest?

But then, beside my sandy feet,
A shell swept up on shore.
The voice's words returned, becoming
Clearer than before.

Your life is like this empty shell;
It has no use at all,
As long as you refuse to hear
The Savior's loving call.

But if you let Him enter in,
Your aimless heart to fill
New life to grant, He'll guide each move
Of the surrendered will

That's why God sent his only Son:
To die, so man might be
Forgiven in His perfect name,
To set his chained soul free.

Then raised Christ back to life again
To finish out God's plan.
No longer death or hell could reign
The heart of transformed man.

What change came over me as all
Was hushed but lapping waves;
What great a comprehension bore
Belief that Jesus saves.

So turning then, to journey home
Before the setting sun,
I, feeling blessed as though my life
Had only just begun,

Had sought for years the flawless shell.
But found that there were none
More beautiful than those indwelled
By God's redeeming Son.

Losing

Your sister won the game again,
Her satisfaction chews
Away at your repulsive pride;
It's difficult to lose.

Your family is cheering on
The team with which you play.
They cry your name, you do your best,
But fail to win today.

A country's chance to win a war
Lies on the men they choose
To strategize and lead them forth,
But someone has to lose.

A greater fight is fought each day
Which every human's in.
The battle even Jesus fought;
The Righteous against sin.

Chained in the prison camp of sin,
Man's race seemed sadly lost.
A perfect sacrifice of blood
For his release would cost

The Son of God His life, but
Willingly He chose that course.
The joy to set us free compelled Him,
He bore no remorse.

No one wants to lose a fight
Or heated argument,
Yet Jesus Christ on earth in poorness
Thirty-three years spent.

He had no friends, was called insane,
He showed the lowest score.
But love and true devotion
Made Him conquer all the more.

So when you feel about to lose,
Don't fail at heart and run.
Recall through Christ the bigger fight
Has already been won.

Remember though one battle's lost,
It is a war you're in,
And sometimes postponed victory,
Secures a better win.

Christ's death secured eternal gain
Where man was at a loss.
Our enemy who'd bound us up
Was conquered at the cross.

So trust the Victor, Jesus, who
Through earth's eyes lost, but knew
The power that restores to life
Would win inside of you.

Not A Cross

No false witnesses,
No betrayer's kiss,
Friend's abandonment,
Murderer's dismiss,

No pretentious robe
For an earthly king,
No reviler's spit
Could to anger bring.

Not a crown of thorns,
Not a soldier's spear,
Not the dragging cross,
Not a bloody tear.

Not an anguished soul
At bearing human's sin,
Not the piercing nails
Feet and hands did pin.

Even not the hour
When the Father's face
Left alone the Crushed,
Dying in our place.

Not a broken heart,
Or tearing like a knife,
Mockery and scorn,
That took our Savior's life.

One word defines His cause;
Death the Maker **chose**,
For love, no thing's more true.
In love the Lord arose.

Not a heavy stone
Not a Roman seal
Not the linen cloths,
Not a lie could steal.

As the roadside rocks
Would have cried His name,
So the rolling stone
His living did proclaim.

The Faith Of Trees

As dawn ascends the sky,
With colorous display,
A grove of yellow aspen trees
Raise up their arms to pray.

Of this they seem aware,
With leafy heads bowed low,
A tinge of autumn in the air
And soon approaching snow.

For birds from far and near
Hold wings outspread to fly
With urge to journey home again
Like strings across the sky.

To everything that flies
'Tis this they seem to call
"Uplift your wings" with urgent cries,
"For summer's turned to fall."

But all the trees stand firm,
And slightly smiling pose,
As if they chuckle then and say
"We have no wings, it shows!"

But we will never fear
As seasons come and go,
For dawning soon another year, will
Melt the grip of snow.

Although our leaves will wilt,
To fall to earth and die,
They will return again in spring,
And sail as kites on high.

So we won't be afraid,
There's One who can prepare
For winter all the things He made,
And tend with loving care

The smallest creatures lives.
He sees and knows their ways;
His eyes are on the sparrows fall,
He hears their songs of praise.

And people, like a leaf,
We vanish in a breeze.
Oh might we learn though life is brief,
To have the faith of trees.

Oftentimes I Pause

Oftentimes I pause,
To listen for the sound
Of gravity that draws
The raindrops to the ground.
Oftentimes I try,
To see the trap that makes
The water of the sky
Unite within the lakes.
Oftentimes I stop,
And wish that pull to touch;
That makes the branches drop
Their apple's steady clutch.
Oftentimes I pause,
To just admire the Source
Of such well-ordered laws
In every unseen force.

Let The Poem Decide

You heave a sigh, this just won't work,
A little irritant.
For stumbling o'er the neatest fit
Long hours you have spent.

Your verses neither flow nor rhyme,
You've tried and tried and tried.
But you forgot the basic step:
To let the poem decide.

You feel disheartened at a glance.
This doesn't look to me
The way correctly written ought,
Or sound like poetry.

By all the regulating points,
Believe you must abide.
Stop fighting with that stubborn beat,
And let the poem decide.

You think by following the rules
And violating none,
With days of tiring work you'll end
Up with a perfect pun.

A day of dictionary search,
Your tongue is getting tied.
Quit pining over needless words
And let the poem decide.

It's driving you insane the time,
And careful thought you've put
Into each idle rhyming scheme,
And stubborn metric foot.

You're so distressed; the stanza lines
Don't properly divide,
Just take a deep, relieving breath
And let the poem decide.

Completing What's Begun

While sitting here
With paper near
and pencil firm in hand,
My thoughts are queer,
For much I fear
You will not understand.

And when I write,
I dread this plight:
With me you won't agree,
And that it might
Be my delight
But not appeal to thee.

So very caught,
I tarry not
To ask of you my friend,
and when I've sought
To hear your thought,
I'm yet to comprehend

Just how I will
Be happy still
To write when some oppose.
With utmost skill,
I'll try until
I've won the hearts of those.

With earnest ways,
And prize the days
To work until its done.
Though much dismays,
It always pays
Completing what's begun.

Empty Mind

The poet sits by a well-lit window,
He plays with his pencil,
And fiddles with his paper,
Perhaps his actions will jog his thoughts.
He gazes out the window,
Wishing there were something written in the sky.

THE
VERSE

'Tis now and then most everyone
Is spurred to write a verse.
It captivates, it's valued fun;
Its themes are quite diverse.

The inner thoughts are breathed to life
Upon the printed page;
Emotions of delight and strife,
Of grief, of joy, and rage.

From sparkling streams that fill the sea,
To twinkling stars on high;
Enthralling lines of poetry
Will come to those who try.

From meadows green and rustling trees,
To lofty mounts that climb;
The words arousing memories,
The core a pleasant rhyme.

Its topics of variety,
With meanings deep; sincere.
That leave the reader soaring free,
And stir ones ears to hear.

Something 'Bout the Verse

There's something in a verse

That cannot be explained,

But all who read it, see and feel it

And are entertained.

There's something 'bout the verse

That cannot be portrayed

By artists' images of life

That paint or pencil made.

There's something in a verse,

The deep and heartfelt thought;

That can express the intimate

When prose alone cannot.

Searching Writer

Come over, come over
And whisper a word in my ear;
Idea recover
The soul of a rover,
In twilight when poems appear.

Come kindly, come kindly,
To quench in the desert mind's thirst.
Idea come find me,
I stumble 'bout blindly
In sandstorm too deeply immersed.

Come over, come over,
Umbrella my arid thought frame.
Idea come hover
With wings of a plover,
And stay, I might give you a name.

A Picture For the Mind

A poem succeeds
Arousing the emotion
Of one who reads,
Evoking the senses,
Building with words;
Like erecting fences,
Leisurely, but clear.

A snapshot there,

A portrait here,

Phrase by phrase

Piecing an image

Together two ways.

A scene for the eyes,

A ring for the ears.

The poet ties

His heart in a box
Wrapped with a bow.
Just one key unlocks.
The power of mind
To a zealous reader
Treasure will unbind.

Value of the Verse

Don't finish jotting down a verse

Dissatisfied and say:

This isn't worth but anything

Except to throw away.

For poetry's a precious thing,

Replaced it cannot be,

The rhyme that tells the heart's aspires

And character of thee.

No Two Alike

Inspiration's like a snowflake
Which haps upon one's open palm.
Its tingling stay is but a second;
A visitation like a balm.

If one's eyes act quick to capture
The contours of the web-like flake,
He might appreciate the detail
A speck of ice or thought can take.

With the beauty of a snowflake,
A new idea flashes by.
A mind might scoff and take no notice,
While a matchless thing lets die.

Soft, a snowflake new is melting
On foreign warmth of human skin.
This one anew will found be never,
Unless one's heart preserves within.

Inspiration's like the snowflakes,
That melting, mental fingers meet.
Absorb before the thoughts diminish;
This priviledged visit won't repeat.

On The Kitchen Floor

Crumbs, more crumbs and spots galore
When I sweep the kitchen floor.
Bread and cake and cookie bits,
Fingernails and cherry pits,
Candy fragments, flour, and hair,
Supper scraps 'neath brother's chair.
Frosting smears and sugar, cheese,
Flying dust that makes me sneeze.
Spills of juice and apple seeds,
Bits of thread and bracelet beads:
Sticky blobs of who knows what,
Crumbled pieces of a nut.
Balls of play-dough, mustard stains,
Everything my fridge contains.
I've been puzzled more and more
By the things that reach the floor.

In Memory of Childhood

Your childhood glimmers somewhere far
Inside your cluttered brain.
The details are forgotten though
Brief moments still remain.

The day you lost a baby tooth,
Or sat on grandpa's lap;
The time you missed a baseball game
Because you took a nap.

When daddy made a tire swing,
The time you wrecked your bike.
The night you just refused to eat
A meal you didn't like.

The evenings by the fireplace,
The snowy winter days.
The time your mother dropped a cake
And puppy licked the glaze.

You went to visit Disneyland,
You met a movie star:
The time you won a contest for
The finest model car.

The day you found a baby bird,
Or fished and caught a sock.
The day you learned to tie your shoe,
Or learned to read the clock.

The time you rode in Uncle's boat,
Your first ride in a plane.
The picnic that was canceled when
The weather turned to rain.

The warmth of every Christmas day
And each Thanksgiving, too.
The taste of winter holidays
In Grandma's chicken stew.

The summer season's laughter, joy,
And eves beside the stream:
Where you in soft and silent grass
Could lie alone and dream.

And even now though many years
Have passed like breezes by,
Your heart's still near the riverside
Beneath the summer sky.

SONS

Trucks and cars and noisy toys
Share the lives of little boys.
Tiny hands with work to do
Make a dandy fix-it crew.
Hammers, nails, a drill and screw;
Saw and lumber, paper, glue.
On the tractor seat again.
Daddy take me for a spin?
Wagon's got a broken wheel,
Better one be made of steel.
Underneath the leaking cart,
Taking something else apart.
Getting big, the boost to start
Growing closer to your heart.

Bandaid Fever

Have to own them just to smell
They ask why; I cannot tell
But when I slip and scrape my knee,
There is a bandaid just for me.

They wonder how the bandaids here
Just always seem to disappear,
For once again the box is gone;
How many, dear, did you put on?

Shopping is the grandest thing;
I feel as I'm the richest king.
Are bandaids written on the list?
I need to stick one on my wrist.

Matters not how they're designed,
I do consider great a find
Bandages of any kind.
I do not care or slightly mind

Whether colored, lined, or plain,
They shall always entertain.
Whether brown or polka dot,
Whether waterproof or not.

Green or purple, blue or red,
I'd never trade for tape instead.
Whether camouflage or pink,
Whether all the wrappers stink,

Whether folded up or creased,
A wrinkled one is one at least.
Whether large or very small,
My hobby's to collect them all.

Rather fingers sore than toes;
Better closer to my nose,
Just to sniff, that scent to keep
Alive for dreams when I'm asleep.

Couldn't wait 'til morning's light,
Bandaids get me feeling right.
Soft and comfy, stretchy too,
If you asked I'd share with you.

I'd gladly own the biggest store
Of them and want a million more.
Nothing's better than to smell,
They ask why; I cannot tell.

For The Love of Elizabeth

Newborn brother cracked his eyes,
A larger world to find.
And human faces quite unknown,
(But one was rather kind.)

While he lay on Mother's breast,
Her heart beset with joy.
"His name is William" Mama grinned
"For he's a handsome boy."

Though he was a helpless babe
At first life-giving breath,
He looked, a lovely image saw;
There stood Elizabeth.

Laughter gleaming in her eye,
A smile across her face;
A charming picture sister made
His mind could not erase.

Soon he'd found how life was hard.
His times did come to cry,
Though Mother could console his hurts,
And Sis would always try.

Time was short as seasons changed,
And infant William grew
To be a toddler as he learned
To walk as others do.

Though he'd siblings six in all
He found a friendship grow,
    And sought to follow everywhere
Elizabeth would go.

    Pleasant was her attitude,
And softest curls to hold;
    From this his heart had seized a dream
That not a soul he'd told.

    Years would alter William's plan.
He failed to understand
    A gentleman in truest love
Had asked for Sister's hand.

    Music of the wedding bells
Proclaimed the answer yes.
    The bridegroom stood to face his love,
Who wore a queenly dress.

    Little brother, clad in white,
Held up the precious ring.
    And though the air was filled with cheer,
His lips were trembling.

    Secretly poor William thought
He chose his bride to be,
    And now his cries, the music broke,
"My sister's leaving me!"

Mother hurried to his side;
"My son why did you wait
      To share your heart?" and down streamed tears
She couldn't palliate.

Empathy the preacher showed;
Kind eyes where pity lay,
      For out of William's problem, there
Did seem no easy way.

Only that he had the choice
To welcome Brother in
      And time would tell of coming springs
He'd fall in love again.

Little Paws and Hooves

A foal and a pup,
Companions for life.
Their earlier years,
With energy rife
A slim cliff avert,
The chicken attack,
The unfriendly skunk,
The neighbor girl's snack,
A bask in the dirt,
A frog in the pond,
A scuffle or two
Would strengthen their bond.
Together grew up
In work and in play,
Were trained by skilled hands
To merit their stay.
An imprint of time
Remains in cement,
When fresh it was poured,
Where puckish feet went.
A memory of prime,
Two prints were redeemed,
How small and wild then,
How innocent seemed.

Phoebe's Little Friend

There are many things a child
can find to do
on a ranch
at only two.

There are tractor rides to catch
When father bales.
Cute request:
"please" never fails.

There are staring contests
to be had with steers,
fence protecting,
twitching ears.

There are riverbanks on which
to sit and splash,
face to smear
with burn pile ash.

There are sticks to throw and
saplings to annoy;
puppy found
a stubborn toy.

There are older brother's boots
to try for size;
hide and seek
with butterflies,

With the garden pea pods piled;
a tasty treat.
Garden hose,
the thirst to meet.

But was Phoebe satisfied
with all this fun?
Not a bit,
but had to stun

Parents by then wandering
away alone.
Soon her foot
slipped on a stone.

But then what did Phoebe spy
In sheltered spot?
Baby fawn
a move made not.

Phoebe coming promptly home,
her calls escaped.
Soon they sighted
what was draped

Gently over tiny shoulders.
"Come and see!"
Mom and Dad
found sympathy.

Three Limericks

There was a young boy who was sick,
A poem worked to heal like a trick.
He laughed such a dread,
He fell from his bed;
The poet was surely a kick!

The maple leaf shouted hooray
As the breeze his branch started to sway,
"I'm leaving my place
To paint the earth's face,"
But the wind blew him into the bay.

There once was a boy in Great Britain
Who'd stolen the neighbor girl's kitten,
The cat got away,
So he had his pay,
Returning home scratched up and bitten.

Rancher's Obligation

They tend their cattle,
A handsome price pay
For love of wild and rugged,
To go the cowboy way.
They learn to saddle
A horse, and to ride,
To shoot a weapon early,
To rope, and brand a hide.
They're trained for battle
Against weathered land.
To benefit, they use it,
The prized that bear their brand.
They know the rattle,
That dangers can strike,
Aware of storms each season,
That no two are alike.
They herd their cattle,
No matter who scorns.
Enough to raise for market
Regard each pair of horns.

The Cowboy Hat

I found a hat,

a cowboy hat

floating down the river.

I reached it with

my walking stick,

caught it by a sliver.

I shook it well

and thumbed the hole

pierced atop I studied,

then lifting on

my head, I smiled,

tipping rim though muddied.

What stories did

this relic hold?

Had the wearer's rifle

a rescue made

from unfair trade

or a neighbor's trifle?

Were Indians

met on the trail,

was there slim escaping;

a horseback ride

warned just in time

when the west was shaping?

Another age,

a held-up stage,

when a horse was hero?

Were cattle grazed

when settlers changed

population zero?

Was there a badge

Worn on the shirt

Below a face so humble,

or did those hands

work farmer's lands,

steering kids from trouble?

Did boots traverse

the acres far

searching for an earning?

Did these keep watch

or join the band

in cattle drive's returning?

Did home they leave

to start afresh,

testing skills of trigger;

to beat all odds,

to cut new routes

when a plot was bigger?

Or lived life old

to mine for gold,

wealthy striking never?

Was this heart killed

that justice stilled

angry crimes endeavor?

Though I may ne'er

the wearer meet

ages up the river,

the head this hat

upon which sat

known is by the Giver.

Cowpokes Code Of Conduct

Every cowpuncher
who puts his boot in the stirrup,
who expects hot coffee
and cakes each morn with syrup,
Must his duty
perform position whichever,
wary of all hazards,
responsibly endeavor.
Prudent judgment,
skilled rifle use can exhibit.
To strike a target able,
His temper must inhibit.
Horse can handle,
and in pursuit will sit steady.
By the drink not taken,
for early rising ready.
Not be vocal,
But words are powered by action.
Wise will keep cows numbered;
the foolish sell a fraction.
Honest, courteous,
whose fellow man first is regarded.
Head kept on his shoulders,
experience not discarded.
Must be watchful,
For rustlers prowl many ranges.
Must have learned the country
to act in sudden changes.
Knows the weather,
That moving cows are not frozen;
Watered cattle are lively:
these are a cow drive's chosen.

The Five Stringed Guitar

Never saw a steamboat,
He never drove a car,
His most prized possession:
A five-stringed guitar.

Brought up on the prairie
By hands that walls upthrust,
His own weight could carry;
Worthy was of trust.

Trailside camps by moonlight
His music brought alive.
He turned from casinos,
Where the crooks connive.

Guarding father's cattle,
A rustler's bullet took.
To dash age-old battles,
His own life forsook.

Fit he was to father
The child he never saw.
Could Ma teach to lasso;
To aim not just draw?

More than daughter's coming
To lift the setting scar,
But Gramps caught her strumming
The five-stringed guitar.

In The Outfit

The head to shield,
The heat will bear,
The wide-rimmed hat
Tips, howdy there!

Domestic duty,
On the trail,
Or helping neighbors
After hail.

Suspenders over
Simple shirt
Assist steer wrestling
In the dirt.

And red bandana
Can't forget
To wipe off forehead
Hard earned sweat.

For working hard
You need no posh,
Just homemade jeans;
a daily wash.

And as for feet,
Shoes never do.
These won't keep snakes
from biting through.

Nor will depart
When waiting jobs
Are cattle chips
In pasture, globs.

A leather pair
of bedside boots,
Complete with spurs
The cowboy suits.

The campfire round
With roping gloves
To tell the tales
A cowpoke loves.

Attire of western
life's enough
For those whose hearts
Are in the rough.

No Trouble Neighbor

His modern ride might be a truck
But his heart is still the same;
To hit the brake when a tractor's stuck
In the ditch, the help to claim.
What damage did the crash provoke?
You will soon be back to work
I left for town 'cause a door hinge broke
Are you not the hardware clerk?
My Ford and chain will pull you out.
Revving engine, in you jump,
A heave a jerk and an okay shout;
Mud-released mounts over bump.
Reliable machine of mine
Yes, she hasn't failed me yet
Much thanks; does a free door hinge sound fine?
Your a pal, come by; no sweat.

Riding

The range stretches out
as far as I can see.
My horse just wants to gallop
forever on with me.

There is no gorgeous sunset,
but the sky
is bluer than the color
of my brother's eye.

We start as if
the thunder's chasing us.
But only hooves are kicking
up thick storm clouds of dust.

I squeeze the reins,
my face set straight ahead
and fancy we are legend
who outrun a slug of lead.

My horse huffs with
the attitude of fire,
the wind unyielding races
as though he'd never tire.

We beat the hawk,
and splash a river through;
I wish to rope a cyclone
as Pecos Bill could do.

Our Paths Have Crossed

We meet again old ranching friend,

Our paths haven't crossed in years.

We seem to bear a bit more wear;

I see lines of smiles and tears.

But how delightful that I might

Pull back on the reins to shake.

Our yarns exchange, some true, some strange;

Still boast in the finest stake.

We'd quarreled some, but far it's from

My heart to revive our spats.

Our roads again have forked my friend,

So long with a wave of hats.

At the Trail's End

The cowboy trail has come to an end
For Grandpa today.
With sorrowful tears we tend
To release our loved
When gone away.

But Grandmother waits in heaven to meet.
He's longing to share
The beauty, that golden street.
His reward pursued,
He's fin'lly there.

His pain has been great, but fleeting, and dim
Near hands that are scarred;
His Savior's were pierced for him.
This path is not long,
It won't be hard.

A horse may be saddled for him there to ride,
A sunset in view;
For only his body died.
He bows at God's throne,
And waits for you.

He wasn't a perfect father to us,
But spared not the rod.
He worked hard, never to fuss,
And with all his heart
He worshiped God.

The Old Red Covered Bridge

Beyond the stream of noisy towns,
The city shortly fades
Into a dusty country road
That winds through quiet glades.

And soon a riverscape appears
Meandering its way
Around the curving countryside,
Whose autumn colors play.

The swooping leaves from outcast limbs
When sudden breezes blow,
Release their hold, and dropping down,
Are carried by the flow.

And swirling round each outcropped rock,
They reach a pleasant scene,
Where lane and riverbank adjoin,
A covered bridge between.

'Twas once the horse and buggy's trail,
'Tis now the auto's street;
The sound of roaring engines by
Instead of trotting feet.

But worn with ruts from constant use,
They rarely travel here,
And so the old red bridge became
A mark of yesteryear.

A spot of calm serenity
Against the ridges yon,
E're watching as the river drifts
Its memories on and on.

Of times when spring adorned the land
With flowers long ago,
And children stopped to run and play
On winter's days of snow.

When summer afternoons were hot,
September eves were warm,
And creatures 'neath the bridges roof
Were safe from every storm.

So when I need a tranquil place
To sit and think a smidge,
I find myself remembering
The old red covered bridge.

Owl's Plight

Owls practice
On a cactus,
Building skills of flight.
Small brother
Follows mother
Under veil of night.

Those older,
Stronger, bolder,
Show ability;
Mice chasing,
Young ones tracing,
Learning all they see.

Come brother
Signals mother
From a nearby limb.
Trust withers
As he dithers;
Petrifying him.

Seems getting
Further spreading
'Tween the parted two.
Dread chaining,
Darkness straining
From the slightest view.

Sole noises:
Family voices'
Reassuring calls.
Owl staying,
Reckless playing;
Time in measure stalls.

But fearing
More the nearing
Sound of heavy wings,
Those waiting
Escalating
Hope so great that stings.

Wings lifting,
Shoves off drifting,
Closing tight his eyes;
Then flapping,
Simply capping
Former flying tries.

Once seeing
What a freeing
Sight of love's embrace,
All beating
Sounds retreating
Triumph on his face.

To Shame the Wise

The foolish things to shame the wise,
And weak the mighty to surprise.
The God of perfect Words is known
To catch the crafty in their own.
A harsh and fearful phrase refute,
With sword-sharp eyes to search for fruit.
The claims of scholars learned destroys,
Rewarding faith of girls and boys.
God uses things men worthless deem
To bring to nothing those which gleam.
Our failures turns He to success,
A stumbling message He can bless.
While choosing to reject the wide,
Swift lips and moving tongue for pride.
The Rock by fool's excuse was skipped,
And over Whom the Jews have tripped.
God's weaknesses the strong outweigh,
His foolish ways with high minds play.
The haughty heart does quick oppose,
But grace toward the humble flows.
He knows that worldly wisdom leads
The man down paths where evil breeds.
And knowledge won't the prudent give
Desire to for their Savior live.
So pleased is He the viewed inane
To use to further heaven's gain.
Christ Jesus when with clouds returns,
The harvest gathers, chaff He burns;
Finds former lost ones overjoyed
The weak and slow his strength employed.

Shooting Star

Did you see that shooting star slice
The cosmic sheet of ice,
Zip the Bootes up,
And splash into the Crater (cup)?

Did you watch the Crater's liquid,
And see what harm it did
Extinguishing a star?
It's surface heat withstood and scar.

Did you see the Lion proud blink?
The Maiden sniffed I think.
But no tears to show
Had the unaffected Crow.

That a brother heaven kindler
Has no more flame to stir,
Snuffed out in a mere
Cold second of a solar year.

Soft

A whisper, a breeze,
A pillow,
A mother's calming squeeze,
A pussy willow,

When waves lick the sand,
A ruffle,
A child in deep sleep's hand,
Inside a truffle,

A baby's lip smack,
Long tresses,
A caterpillar's back,
When peace supresses.

A cumulus sky,
Rose petals,
A lemon merengue pie,
How lake mist settles.

Butterflies, a leaf
On water
One's pass to end of grief,
Cheek of a daughter,

Sentimental hearts,
A feather,
Where ocean ends, sky starts,
Blue comes together.

An uplifting word,
What's mellow,
The flight of a bird,
Moon rising yellow,

The tail of a storm,
A midnight candle,
A blanket that is warm,
A farewell tearful.

Children's Words

There's no one like a child
To write a children's book.
Adults by wealth are wiled
To press the perfect look.

Experience is small,
But fresh to young appeals
To kids that care at all
To know another feels

The same about a hope,
A problem, or a goal;
While famous authors grope
For language's control.

The younger mind is quick
To speak straight from the heart;
Professional pens stick
In adjectives, not art.

A child's discovery
In passion comes alive,
Expressions echo free,
An open world's the drive.

A man may write with knack
An epic in the wilds,
But words will not spring back
As charming as a child's.

I've Heard A Song

I have heard a song of praise
Not from voices in the church,
Not where every tither pays,
Or where vain religions search.

I have heard my Savior blessed
In the bowing of a knee
How the creatures do it best:
Beaver, ant, and fish, and bee.

Giving glory to His name,
No deceptive word can slim.
Even tiny flowers claim
Their identity in Him.

Where the deep sea whales converse,
Butterflies emerge on wing,
Where the podded seeds disperse,
There is glory to the King.

Where in peaceful wooded glades
All the wind-filled trees rejoice,
And the rumbling ocean fades
Out all doubting with its voice.

In the twinkling heaven spheres,
In a rainbow o'er a field;
To each living thing which hears
Is His majesty revealed.

And those joyful words they sing
Endlessly, sound quite like this:
When in harm'ny mingling
Like a river's raindrop kiss.

Sing a song to God that's new,
Beautiful in holiness;
What the people failed to do
Roaming in the wilderness.

All the gods fall at His feet,
All the earth is trembling.
He, on heaven's mercy seat
Judges right in everything.

Maker who surpasses You?
Match can none Who does no wrong.
People give Him all that's due;
Honor Him in worship song.

Let all nations fear His name,
His salvation be declared;
Why the servant Jesus came,
Why from death He was not spared.

Mountains blow a trumpet blast,
Heavens ring triumphantly.
Timbrel sound as when God cast
Egypt's riders in the sea.

He is coming, coming soon.
Vain and earthly goods will fall,
Needing no more sun or moon;
Justly will His truth judge all.

Yes, the Lord forever reigns!
Praise Him even barren land.
This is what our tune remains:
All else fades, but His Words stand.

If that's what the creatures do
When at Jesus feet all day,
May my heart be humble too,
May my knees be bowed to stay.

Ocean's Daughter

In the harbor,
On the water,
On her starboard,
"Ocean's Daughter."

Tresses tangled,
Clothing tattered,
Grime has strangled,
Body battered.

Contents taken,
Youth is over,
Friends forsaken,
One-leafed clover.

Eyes are dripping,
Life is draining,
Faint and tipping,
Fate is gaining.

She exposes
Brutal fury.
Sea reposes,
All grow leery.

Yet, oh mother,
You dealt gently.
Stronger brother
Grave-bound sent ye.

In the harbor,
On the water,
Sagging starboard,
"Ocean's Daughter."

To Tell the World

A message I heard has opened my eyes
To all of the lost and hurting ones' cries.
A great many souls meet death every day,
And never were told of God's perfect Way.
A calling to act, each soldier of Christ,
To those whom the world has never enticed.
We're seeing at home and places abroad
Where few of the Savior's followers trod.
In countries possessed by evil and fraud
They're worshiping not the only true God.
In countries where food is hard to afford,
They're hungry for truth; they don't know the Lord.
That Jesus was bruised and died for our sin,
And God loves all men, has time and again
Been preached to the church that turns a deaf ear,
And not reached the ones so willing to hear.
Our churches we fund with lovely designs,
When over the sea, they worship in shrines.
Those souls who have searched, and all their lives missed
The truth that a God who loves does exist.

The freedom is scarce in regions afar,
We often don't see how priv'leged we are
To live in a place where no one is made
To give up their faith in Christ or be slayed.
No access have they, nor Bibles to read,
'Til someone who knows is willing to lead.
We lift up the prayer that someone will go.
If no one is sent, then how will they know?
And how will they hear if no one will teach?
All Christians are called the world to reach.
In vast places Christ is not even named!
Oh, may we reach out and be unashamed.
To all of the lands where Islam is spread,
I see all the souls of Christ being led
In fearless attempt, in deepest desire,
The hopeless and lost to pull from the fire.
Who work 'til His love is taken among
God's every nation, people, and tongue.
To see a revival sweep across seas,
Not resting 'til all are brought to their knees.
Dear Jesus create a passion that glows
On fire for You, with heartache for those;
To see them be saved, and make this our plea:
That if it's Your will, Lord Jesus, send me.

PAPER

It's something anyone can use
In almost any way.
Its list of roles has not an end
For work and even play.

Yes, paper is a handy thing
To take on ev'ry trip,
Provided that you never leave
Without a paper clip.

Some paper towels, paper plates,
And cups of paper too;
It's great to know the valued things
That paper does for you.

There's scraps of paper round your desk,
A folded plane or hat,
A sheet of notes in harmony;
There's room 'cause paper's flat.

And yet it starts to clutter space;
The shelves are piled with books.
Still paper holds a recipe
That aids the finest cooks.

It profits in a building plan,
It tells the latest news.
It's made into a little box
That keeps a pair of shoes.

It lies around in wait for use,
It's used and used once more.
We even glue it to our walls,
And tape it to the door.

The artist knows of paper well,
The author grips it dear.
For paper has a place in life,
And now it's very clear

That paper's quite a lot of things,
All sorts of shapes and hues.
But you, my friend, should ponder how
You're privileged it to use.

So having paper makes me glad
And not forget to be
Extremely grateful to the One
Who wrought its source: the tree!

NUTTY

For whether on the forest floor
Or high up in a tree,
It's chattering and nuts galore;
Content as life could be.

Away they scamper round and round
About their busy ways,
And with precision turn the ground
Into an acorn maze.

A clump of wiggly fun and fur,
Whose quick and agile feet
Will scurry off in much a blur
If danger chance to meet.

Without a single anxious thought,
The ground is far below.
Those squirrelly critters, rarely caught,
Are always on the go!

THE TINY CLOUD

Much like a feather trailing by,

A smudge of white,

A cloud in sight,

So wispy in the massive sky.

It ceased to move, and clung with fear.

To fade away,

Before its day,

For breezes left it but a smear.

Yet though 'twas firm to linger there,

A drift of wind

Had left it thinned,

And soon it vanished in the air.

THE OLD
SEA CAPTAIN

An old sea captain left the earth,
But what he's written lingers still
With certain taste of mirth,
With charming skill.

The works reveal his attitude
And what his outlook was on life;
Although in solitude,
He, joy was rife.

He told the tales that seamen do,
But with an even greater feel.
And they he surely knew
A heart would steal.

He told of most the peaceful days
Of when his searching soul felt free,
And what it's like to gaze
Continu'lly

Upon the open sea and sky,
And go adrift between the two.
His want was here to die
Amid the blue.

He told of stormy times as well,
Of moaning wind that caught the mast
When rocking on a swell,
As billows passed.

He told of feelings, smells, and sights,
And ways of reading signs at sea;
The use of astral lights:
A sailor's key.

And his imagination brought
An epic tune to all he said.
To know all seas was taught
And where they led.

He left a remnant of himself
To be revealed to you and me
Upon his cabin shelf;
His legacy.

And yes, he got his only wish,
To honor what this seaman wrote,
His grave with wand'ring fish,
His soul afloat.

THE EYES

I stumbled once upon a verse,

    And paused to ponder what it said.

That perfect ballad though 'twas terse

    So stirred my heart and thus it read:

The mind does not deceive the eye,

    But rather eyes induce the mind.

To cast them on mere sin, not I,

    For one would better off be blind.

SEASON OF WINTER

When fallen leaves compel the snow
To hurry on its way,
    And dismal clouds conceal the sun
That lit the hours of May,

    The chilly winds unveil their fright
Upon the barren trees,
    While creatures hide in sleep secure
And wait for earth to freeze.

    Beneath a suit of sparkling ice,
And frosty silver flakes,
    'Til spring dissolves its hold again,
And March's morning breaks.

I Will Return

The steamboat whistle shrieks its blow,

And quickened feet

Traverse by morning's lamps aglow

Throughout the street.

A black umbrella shelters two

From pouring rain.

A soldier knows his words are few,

And time his pain.

He gently looks into the eyes

Of whom he loves,

The teary eyes to dry he tries

With urgent gloves.

A shaking hand he aches to hold,

His inward war,

And trembling lips with fear and cold

He can't ignore.

The girl who's going from his arms,

Not long ago

The tiny babe who won with charms

All Daddy's know.

But greater cause pulls at his heart,

A kindled flame,

A loyal spirit men can't part

With calls his name.

He, summoned by a greater power

Than you or I,

Cannot retreat to watch an hour.

But should he die?

I love you, father, please don't leave;

Her silent plea,

And rubs her face with soiled sleeve.

How grieved is he.

But in the rhythm of their hearts

His last farewell

He utters, with a wave departs,

The worst can't tell.

How many willing bodies died

For reasons right,

How many fell there flag beside

In dark of night.

For who fought some do not recall,

But how they fought.

Their choice to in the battle fall

For self was not.

Look, when the captain shouts ahoy

Out from the stern.

When summer breathes her air of joy

I will return.

The able service due my land

Can never lack.

'Til freedom reigns as God has planned,

I won't be back.

But when the torch of liberty

Begins to burn,

And when our banner high you see,

I will return.

The Kingdom of Light

I wandered about in the caverns of sin,
The pathways once pleasant to me.
Inhaling the fumes and the soot on my skin,
The darkness my sole company,

And merciless labor no longer sufficed
My hunger to go my own way.
The glittering stones and the gold once enticed
But now only brought me dismay.

Withdrew I my pick from the unyielding rock,
Then threw it in utter disgust.
A tunnel caved in, and shown after the shock
A channel of light through the dust.

Its newness compelled and I cautiously strode
For promising difference in life.
But finding the exit of my soul's abode,
My boss blocked the way with a knife!

I'd always obeyed him and never gave thought
To ask for more wages or light.
My contract was lifelong; I signed it with hot
Fingers which only knew night.

He governed my every movement and want,
He told me I never could leave;
While darkness unknown by me closed in to haunt
'Neath light I just had to receive.

The threats my employer made failed to obstruct
My light-thirsty heart for fresh air.
I darted from swipes, from his flying knife ducked,
Emerged I to find freedom there.

I lost all remembrance of old hankering.
A friend in his scarred hand took mine.
I joined with those saved the employ of a King,
Who wrought by the Spirit's joy shine.

Delivering us from the darkness' power,
Partakers with saints of light made.
Jehovah was pleased in Golgotha's devour;
That His glory might be displayed

In raising the Son of his love, with that power
His kingdom to we are conveyed.

Colossians 1:12-13

How Flight Began

The Orville Brothers,
Kitty Hawk,
A spaceward race
Against the clock.
It all began
when flightless man
Decided he
would someday span
The sky on wing,
And sail the air.
The birds he saw,
He envied their
Ability
To brave the heights.
Tall tales were told
On winter nights
Of days when man
Would heaven share,
In little time
Go anywhere.
Ideas bloomed
When these were gone,
But legacy
Is what lives on.
Through all delays
And tragedies,
Men spent their lives
To ride the breeze.
One day their wildest

Dreams came true,
Relentless work
Brought flight to you.
And since the
Orville brothers flew,
The want to transport
Faster, grew.
The news of planes
Swept through the land.
A little child
Would gaze and stand,
And point a finger
Heavenward:
That loud machine
Looks like a bird!
His mother'd giggle
Then explain:
This speed advance
Will be our gain.
She spoke the truth,
For World War 1
Would reign the sky,
And fly the gun.
Communication time
Would drop,
Air travel would
Rise to the top.
Today, with jets,
With cash we race
The open world
To anyplace.

Complaining when
Delay occurs,
Or when airsickness
Senses blurs.
While probably
Not giving thought
To how the flight
Beginners fought
Against the scoffers
Of their quest,
Who claimed they should
Live in a nest;
And how some gave
Their lives away,
That we'd enjoy
Airplanes today.

November Visions By Moonlight

Old man's beards curl
Around bare limbs,
Branched brooks 'neath purl

And daylight dims.

Stabbed by tree twigs,
The painless moon;

Like smoke from cigs,
Grey clouds balloon.

Westward chills blow
To chase the sun
Under earth's toe.

Bright hues make fun
Of the dead ground.

A wet-note drops
To be stream-drowned.

Like spinning tops,
Trees shed scales whirl
And lightly land;

Like laughs of girls,
Small waves expand.

A Special Tree

A wise old tree
With locks of moss,
Ten decades high,
One-tenth across,

He keeps the spot
Where once a seed
Was tended very
Well indeed.

His brothers downed
By builder's ax,
Built temple walls,
And sold for tax.

Though father went
Onto the sea,
A vessel proud,
Was lost to be.

While mother tree
Was left to rot,
Fell in a storm
And found was not.

Still stands the tree,
The lonely tree,
And overlooks
The silent sea.

His heart recalls
At staring down,
His family
Before the town.

To part with earth
The last he'll be.
The arms that hold
Eternity

Across that wooden
Cross will span;
The tree will be
Part of God's plan

When every sin
Ungodly men
Committed will
Be payed for in

The moment when
Christ took the blame,
His life's blood gave
Lost souls to claim.

Untold his job
Is best of all,
When up the axman
Comes to fall.

Not A Living Soul

For there is not a living soul
Who can fulfill
A perfect life upright and whole;
Whose sins are nil.

Aye, there is not a godly man
Whose lips are still,
And keep his temperament he can
From growing ill.

For there is not a being just,
Who never makes
The choice corrupt to follow lust
And grave mistakes.

Yet he assumes false decencies
Could earn the cost
Required to save, but God decrees
That man is lost.

For not a human man could pay
Redemption's price,
For Jesus' blood's the only way;
His sacrifice.

The Lamb condemned His life to lose,
Hence to bestow
Salvation for the ones who choose
Christ's way to go.

And Jesus' rise to life alone,
The path revealed
To passage free before His throne;
Soul's death repealed.

Timmy's Rescue

Timmy hears the lonely howling
Break the silence of the night.
Stops he not to think a minute,
Tip-toeing into the bright

Softness of the moonlit outside,
Being sure he isn't heard.
Eerie blinking eyes and shadows
Underneath tree limbs are stirred.

Gazing out into the darkness,
As it inches to its prey,
Whining, crying for deliverance.
Timmy feels compassion weigh

On his heart for what poor critter
Makes that sad, recurrent sound.
Searching briskly through the thickets,
Finds a coyote on the ground.

Just a baby, helpless orphan,
Cold and lost and hungry too,
Backs away in fearful trembling.
What does little Timmy do?

Reaches down with care and kindness,
Lifts in arms the whimpering pup.
But returns he to discover
Both his parents waiting up,

Bearing questioning expressions.
Timmy cannot much but freeze,
Gesturing toward his treasure,
Won't you let me keep him please?!

The Great Physician

You need no appointment
To see the Great Physician,
No cost for examines,
Salvation is His mission.

By scores men in wonder
This Healer's clinic enter,
Are drawn by compassion
Where their concerns are center.

Upon diagnosis, though,
Many are offended,
Refusing best treatment,
Addictions have befriended.

The gross alleys wander
To satisfy lusts passions,
When struck with diseases,
Psychiatrist's trust fashions.

The problem avoided
In this fake doctor's folder,
The symptoms pill covered;
Forget you're getting older.

Then follows depression
As visioned satisfaction
Withdraws like the ocean,
Compelled are to take action

One's name make remembered,
With causes he's full taken
Which reap sudden products,
But by small storms are shaken.

A dark day one happens
To pass by the Physicians,
A clinic outliving
All tide-swept superstitions.

With qualm he approaches
And glances in the window.
A cure he is seeking
From death's impending shadow.

There's nobody waiting,
And none lined up for healing,
Just the Doctor playing
An instrument with feeling.

His instrument's quickly
Aside set at His sighting
The man outside, lonely,
Receives a smile inviting.

That once he'd rejected
The truth seems not to bother,
The Great Physician raises
His hands up to the Father.

His thanks for this lost one
Returning to Him hopeless,
This person overwhelming,
Who cries out for forgiveness.

I'll take any treatment
No matter how disgusting,
If it can make me better,
I'm finished with my lusting!

Your faith is but little
Replies the Great Physician,
Believe that I can save you
With heart of true contrition.

The cure's not appealing;
Earth's hardships here beginning.
Your cross take up and follow,
Denying self, Life winning.

Free Verse

I'd always so specific been,
I liked the rules to perfect keep.
So frustration mounted when
Literary lines would leap

Instead of creep along the page.
A purling rivulet in prime
Would jerk and grow a beard of age
Along a span of imperfect time.

When summer warblers howled and barked
On limbs of ivory,
That first my ears their music marked,
They translated cacophony.

But unprepared I rode a poem
That landed in a verdant plain,
And bid me look and find the home
Of a caterpillar sane.

His weaving undisturbed cocoon,
Knowing humbly his lot to be
Shortly with gently passing moon,
A butterfly let free.

Trivial Efforts

You meet a poet,
You pun a bit,
You use your knowledge,
He adds wit.

You catch an actor
To autograph
A card. Your homage
Wins a laugh.

You boast to buddies,
They slight each feat
By naming deeds
They fail to meet.

An artist visit,
His art admire.
He answers each thing
You inquire.

A pilot's handshake,
An airshow at;
A baseball star
Gives you a bat.

You meet an athlete,
He wears you out
With training
All he talks about.

You meet a singer,
Your love inflate
Of music you
Don't view so great.

Receive a ticket,
Policeman find
Is not a monster,
Rather kind.

A firefighter once
Saved your life.
A hunter bought you
A skinning knife.

The President glances
Once your way,
A prickly feeling
Starts to play.

You greet a soldier,
And shine support;
Of words expressive
You feel short.

Attend a banquet
With king and queen,
Your awe wears
As you wisdom glean.

You meet a person
From distant land;
In language
Neither understand.

You're left unaltered,
Though strange to thought,
You've found these, too
Are perfect not.

You meet the Maker,
His Son receive,
And your heart empty
He won't leave.

What's In It For You?

The life of one is lonely
And sad, though it may have seemed free,
Who always said
What's in it for me?

A bachelor's life is haunted
By kids he now wishes he had.
What's in it for me
Does not make a dad.

A millionaire used people,
Ignoring his conscience's plea,
Who always thought
What's in it for me?

A marriage has been broken,
The real reason most do not see.
They always said
What's in it for me?

A homeless man is begging,
Who shunned responsibility.
He seeks from life
What's in it for me?

A woman lost her parents,
She's bitter and cold as can be.
She always thought
What's in it for me?

An Individual joyful
Though His hands, feet, and side were pierced through;
He always thought
What's in it for you?

The Scar Of Anger

The mouth blurts out a word,
A hurtful word,
A cutting word,
The ears it fell on numbed;
Some fight returned,
Ignorance learned,
But angry blasts succumbed.

The heart from which the words,
The hurtful words,
And cutting words,
Were traced, was damaged once.
A partly mended
Wound opened
By someone's spite or brunts.

The mouth shouts out a word,
A hurtful word,
A cutting word,
When memory is pricked
Of slicing treatment
In wrath's heat
That to the same would addict.

A quiet answer turns
All wrath away,
Those bitter chains,
Broken by Jesus' peace.
Be still and know
That God can go
To storms and make them cease.

Accountability

The last I knew, this land was free.
So I can do just as I please?!
If this is your philosophy,
Then you have caught the world's disease.

When self gets loose, allowed to reign,
Then no one matters much but me.
No! let the only truth remain:
United under God is free.

Christian Calling

When we don't do
What we ought to,
When we know it,
But forgo it;
Undermining,
We're resigning
Our position
Of remission.
Our Physician
Has a mission,
Our decision
To petition
Must be willing
And fulfilling.

As Jesus Did

To have the final word
As Jesus did,
Would be abused
By a common kid.

He opened up His mouth
In unfailing speech,
And it was coveted
The means with which he'd teach.

To shame the haughty man,
The rich and wise;
To discern what's beneath
A sincere guise.

To speak the winning word,
A puffed heart rid,
To imperfect man
Is a hopeless bid.

Could he pick up the cross,
Harsh jeers amid?
His life place in their hands
As Jesus did?

The Greatest Love

The love of God is nothing
Like the love of man;
God's love meant giving up His Son
To carry out His plan.

While man dreams of his lover
In sentimental mist,
The One who never lived for self
Betrayed is with a kiss.

Man seeks to meet his wishes
With what is love he claims,
But Jesus in Gethsemane
God's will His mindset frames.

This same One is forsaken
By Father on the cross,
Though now Christ's life seems wasted, He
Brings mankind's love to dross.

To man love is a feeling,
To God, purely an act.
If you desire God's definition,
God is love, that's fact.

If three things could determine
What love is meant to be,
The life, and death, and rise of Christ
Are perfect proof for me.

To follow Christ's example
Is why my life I live,
To help another find this love
He was so quick to give.

A man indwelled by Jesus,
For this love strive he does,
But Jesus lived the greatest love
There ever is and was.

How's Your Journey?

Are you walking on the road that Jesus walked
Or just trying to do better than before?
I recall the Savior's words when He was mocked,
Do you know for your redemption what He bore?

He said Father forgive them, for they know not what they do!
For the greatest mockers of His name, Christ died for me and you.
May this cause us to embrace His love and mercy more and more.

Are you sitting at his feet from day to day,
And relying on His strength in battle's wake?
Are you keeping His command to watch and pray,
And fulfilling Christ's commission for His sake?

Can you prove, O soldier, that your armor's good?
When the devil comes to tempt will you withstand?
Are you eating daily from the Father's food?
Are your movements guided by His loving Hand?

Are you listening for His answer when you call?
Are you waiting for His voice your heart to lead?
God remembers in His plan though large or small,
Every detail in your life, your every need.

Did you know, O soldier, you are not the first
To be ridiculed in the Narrow Way?
But when love responds with good to those who've cursed,
What a guilty shame does sinner's deeds repay.

Do you know, O soldier, Jesus came before;
He knows everything you're feeling in this fight.
Tell, His message will be spreading more and more,
'Til the darkness is drowned out by Jesus' light.

War Among The Planets

There is a war among the planets,
Upon which stars and earth can't gaze.
The moon has been unfettered.
All hearts have turned to granites.
They shall not rest a single phase,
'Til net they worlds unlettered.

The lunar edge is chipped and swollen,
But cycle to once more reverts;
Displaced warship returning,
To wake the sea waves sullen.
But adversary spots and skirts
All sides with torches burning.

Denying right of light from heaven
To liberate his ghostly frame;
His heart sold to subjection,
Outnumbered one to seven.
Yet holds the sky, the buffs to shame
Of commonplace rejection.

Worn-out material he's labeled,
An easy catch and trial should come.
But watch his surface waxing,
That closing circle fabled;
Dims neighbor stars, outshining some,
Although his flight is taxing.

There is a war among the planets.
Now weapons must be put to use,
Destructive minds un-thwarted,
Wants quick to sate as bandits'.
If moon be captured, faces noose;
This price would leave foes shorted.

What chance remains of his surviving?
His vuln'rability is keen.
A ship without a rudder,
And cannon-less, wind driving
To combat, wedged two rocks between,
With no cry left to utter.

Would not the act of sea consuming
Be yet a finer cup of ends?
When moon's reflection touches
The waves might foam, entombing.
Eternity here sailor spends,
Hand rotting, seaweed clutches.

His melancholic sheen grows dimmer,
As over sidling his sphere,
Like fingers suffocating,
The purple haze's threats steam grimmer.
It's vaporizing hissings blear
Fate's plan of dissipating.

But hope! Earth's eyelids ope to needy.
Her yonder shape refreshes quite
Like rising tide a tremor;
Bonds, drawing up a treaty.
The terms of which might heal the blight
Moon's curbing served as stemmer.

The flag of truce waves antebellum.
Would enemy conditions meet,
Or meteoric showers
Fire, using warfare seldom
Up conjured just for smooth defeat,
At which a tiger cowers?

The pendulum of timeless ticking,
That past a pleasant moment slips,
As sunlight earth starts blocking;
The clock a moment sticking
In anxious bloody moon eclipse.
Ghost mediator's walking.

A ray jets out, the sun's emerging
To center hold of galaxy,
Whose torrid vastness glowers
On radicals for purging
The minds of spontaneity,
And supernat'ral powers.

The planets blinded, weapons vanish.
The moon attains horizon whole,
His night parole ignited.
Though vision is outlandish,
The bend-less rules cannot control.
He's even been invited

To share with stars the ocean covers,
Whose once again familiar rote
Stirs shellfish in their dreaming.
Between horizons hovers,
A weary word's worth laden boat.
His foremost trait redeeming:

Assumed identity of mortal,
His eyes allured by simple land,
Lips round in thought grow wider;
New life at mental portal,
A verse-filled pencil in his hand,
Experience reciter.

His cooler edge may be a myst'ry,
But not where inspiration lacks.
Romanticism christens
The browning page of hist'ry.
The moon on constant move leaves tracks,
And speaks to he who listens.

(For explanation see next page)

Explanation of "War Among the Planets"

I dedicate the following explanation of the poem "War Among the Planets" to my dad, who first suggested my writing of it. I direct it to friends, family, and others who have or wish to read the poem. I write this clarification considerate of your desire to comprehend what lies under the physical face of the lexical meaning of the words; knowing that I too would become lost in the tangled film of figurative language (were it not for the fact that I composed the lines). In this explanation, the literal and symbolic meaning of the verses will be defined.

The poem unfolds dramatically with a proclamation of war, but confusion is borne with the presentation of the objects involved: planets, stars, and moon (so far). Bear in mind that the head and body of the poem is the device, symbolism. Nearly everything mentioned has symbolic worth. Now, what each of these objects stand for must be clarified by exploring the relevance of their historical counterparts.

The nineteenth century in England awoke to a poetic revolution, of which the acclaimed romantic poet, William Wordsworth, played tremendous part. The stark contrast between the prevalent neoclassic view of poetry and that of newly emerging romanticism, he enlightened in his Preface to Lyrical Ballads. Lyrical Ballads is a collection of works composed by Wordsworth and his friend, Samuel Taylor Coleridge, in which they each express their strong desire to depart from the rules and restrictions placed on man and his mind by neoclassicism. Embarking on a voyage to exhume a place that would free the poet from the trends of objectivity, specifics, and the belief that writing only holds the purposes of teaching and informing, these two men pressed emphasis on the imagination, nature, the commonplace, and spontaneity. In essence, romanticism was not the addition of a new genre to literature, but the introduction of an innovative outlook, attitude, and channel of expressing life through the development of less restrained artistic forms.

Key words describe the features of romantic poetry: individualism, subjectivity, emotion, imagination, nature, synthesis, simplicity, mystery, melancholy, spontaneity, commonplace, and the supernatural. The order in which these characteristics are listed does not elevate any one over the other, although some of the ingredients are used in larger amounts. All of these aspects are individuals of the whole of the romantic movement, and (for the most part) in this poem.

The planets introduced in line one are symbolic of the neoclassicists (or neoclassicism in general), the stars; contemporary artists of the period, earth; the arts, and the moon, on careful consideration can be discovered to represent romanticists (or romanticism in general). The war addressed in line one is the poetic revolution. Why is the war among the planets when it seems the moon is in opposition? The moon (romanticism) is portrayed as a convict being released from prison. What offenses had he committed in his former life? Or, rather, was he falsely accused? At any rate, an authority saw it fit to free him, and his liberation ignites a strong opposition.

The war zone encompasses the entire solar system (or all people aware of the disagreement between romantic thought and neoclassical rule). The refusal of the stars and the earth to "gaze upon" (the fight) suggests their neutrality. The stars, (contemporary artists of the period) concerned that their popularity runs the risk of being damaged, do not wish to state an opinion of their standing in the midst of this revolt. Earth (art itself) was brought about by the merging of emotions (predominately positive) rather than discorded feelings. In the beginning, God, the greatest Artist wrought the greatest art of all time when He spoke light into being.

"And God saw the light, that it was good..." Genesis 1:4. The creation pleased the Maker. Perfection was the first masterpiece. Therefore, earth shuns discord.

The French Revolution was one event that greatly inspired the emergence of romantic thought. The moon is released. Granting hearts to the planets that harden like granite stone at this moment, personifies neoclassicism. The word "phase" in line five, refers to the component in the cycle of the literal moon, as compared to the small space of time the planets (neoclassicists) will not wait to pursue the moon.

Line six expresses the grim attempt of those who consider new thought to be uneducated and a threat, to bring it under their control. This is the neoclassical mindset. Remember that romanticism and neoclassicism are processes of thought. The goal of the poem is not to create monsters and victims, but to relate in an epic tale, the birth of a revolution in thought and art.

Novel thought emerges weakly, accepted by few at first, left to advocate for support. Being in the minority, the liberated moon suffers under the judgements of others, with little encouragement. Its incompleteness is denoted by the words "chipped and swollen", which describe the condition of the waxing gibbous moon, just after the first quarter.

The following line seems to deny that romanticism is new, but that it is rather reemerging: "...cycle to once more reverts". The moon returns to its pre-detention lifestyle. Since the largest piece in the pie is nature, which has existed since the world was created, an element of resurfacing cannot be ignored. Romanticism's goal is to revive the beauty of the natural and common by observing rarities that lie under the veil of the physical with original language use. The picture of the moon adds the trait of timelessness.

A metaphor portrays romanticism in line three of stanza two as a returning warship that has been displaced. A ship that was either lost or discharged, never to combat in the battle, returns home without honor. This is the state of beginning thought. Honor must be merited.

As line three flows into line four, the recurring symbol of water is introduced. Water symbolizes language's creativity. At this point, we discover the sea body as being "sullen" (stagnant and nearly lifeless). This "dead sea" effect alludes to the result that the moon's absence or a discontinuation of its cycle would have on tidal activity. But, "sent to wake the sea waves sullen", returning to its cycle, the moon again (or starts) influencing the movement of the waves (creativity with words) and beckons back the essential flora and fauna (diversity in language) which could not survive in the "dead" ocean.

The effect of a vessel (moon compared to ship) gliding over still waters, arousing even the smallest bit of wave activity, does not go unnoticed. The "adversary" (neoclassicism) alert, and quick to perceive the change, reacts by surrounding this newcomer with "torches burning", or by keeping the novel movement in check. Words are the biggest weapon. Threats may be thrown and exchanged.

The foes are in denial, in line one of stanza three, of the "right of light from heaven", or the sun's authority to free "liberate" the moon's "ghostly frame". The sun, being symbolic of life and inspiration (the source of life of every thought), seemingly could not prevent itself from giving a "bright side" to the moon.

The moon's heart is "sold to" or infatuated with subjection, a basic ingredient in the substance of romanticism. Opposite of objection, the neoclassical approach to literature and art, subjection causes the reader to be subject to the feelings and personal views of the author expressed in his unique style. it could be said of all the heavenly bodies in the solar system (and universe) the moon is most personal in his wearing somewhat human facial characteristics.

The moon appears to be engaging in this fight alone "outnumbered one to seven". Seven is the number of the planets, (excluding earth and pluto, the dwarf planet) and the lucky number of the neoclassicists who presume all things are under the spell of precision. Seven, also the Biblical number of completion, shows the exaggeration of "perfected" neoclassical thought and the exclusion of anything irregular.

Despite the moon's apparent position on the losing side, he does not relinquish his small grip and placement in the sky: "...holds the sky...". A depiction of endless opportunities and possibilities, the sky operates as an indirect and unseen ally, sustaining the moon on its journey. So the moon grasps opportunity tight, his witty weapon; inspiration, to put to shame the "buffs" or supporters of the rejection of the commonplace.

Commonplace is the romantic writer's tendency of choosing common objects, scenes, and happenings as themes for their compositions. It may be agreed that commonplace plays the second largest role after subjection in creating the literary attitude of romanticism. Commonplace contributes the subject and setting for most poet's works of such. Commonplace use is the reality of the idea that unordinary and uncommon things can stem from the ordinary, or an uncommon approach may be taken in description. New perspectives and new beauties can be drawn from natural experience. Neoclassicism rejects this belief with their regulating artificial beauty. Hence the closing phrase of stanza three "...buffs...of commonplace rejection".

To an earthly observer, the matter of which the moon is comprised may appear worn-out, ragged, beaten, and useless. Likewise, the "material" produced throughout and after the romantic movement, because of its simple, ordinary, and subjective extremities, may have been termed trite or useless. Since its influence was minor at the time, an easy fulfillment of the movement's elimination could be sensed. (Note the pun on "movement"; the romantic movement and the movement of the moon). But just as the lit side of the moon waxes or increases according to its cycle, so grew gradually the popularity of this original outlook taking creative excursions.

The word "fabled" in line four of stanza four, refers to the belief that this movement would not continue or expand. It also alludes to the idea that the moon is only a sphere when it is full. Of course, the moon waxes and brightens, dimming neighbor stars. The disappearing stars (contemporary artists) are succeeded by the light of the romantic achievements. What other artists have attained becomes dim in comparison to the brilliant ideas produced in the romantic mind, which in the written word progress even in dark opposition.

So far, the "war" spoken of is solely a declaration, as countries proclaim before the initial battle. The first quartet of stanzas just examined in this poem could be called "Revolution's Proclamation". Stanza five presents preparation for battle.

The restatement of the first line of the poem at the beginning of stanza five, intensifies and foreshadows the imminence of violent retaliation. With "destructive minds" the foes of the moon inspect their weaponry and devise their strategy of warfare. Their schemes remain "un-thwarted": so far unbeatable, unable to be tricked or reasoned with. As money-hungry bandits pillaging a vulnerable town, the neoclassic vengeful desires will not be easily appeased. If neoclassicism wins the war, which seems highly probable, it is beyond a doubt that it would endeavor to utterly remove its opposition from the universe forever.

How would this leave their desires "shorted" as the last line in stanza five states? Even if the neoclassicists rid all of the rebel's influence, remnants of the novel expression could not be eradicated. The foe's reputation would be marred in the gruesome process. "Killing" the moon would not eliminate the impact already made on the earth and stars, (language, creativity, people) and therefore, could not gratify the demands of the enemy.

A hyperbole is a figure of speech used in poetry and other

literature, designed to exaggerate a point for effect. This overstatement is employed to heighten the maliciousness of the neoclassicist's and their doctrines.

Stanza six opens with an inquiry which questions the moon's capability to withstand the aggressiveness and unquenchable greediness of his adversary. He is again compared to a handicapped ship, to demonstrate his "vulnerability". This vessel has no means of defense against foe: "cannon-less", without a rudder, abandoned to the merciless driving of the wind and waves. These cause it to be "wedged two rocks between", still attempting to buffet the oncoming adversary.

In his massive fear, the moon fails to send out a message of distress. Not allowing a blow to his pride (criticism) to harm his potential and effort, even when caught in tough place, the romanticist used his writing to expel his problems, trying to solve them through reason. The lamentation of some lyricist's of this era was that life was discovered to be too short to achieve set goals through trial and loss (similar to William Wordsworth's loss of family members). Many compositions bear the worries and questions of the day, accompanied by possible peace that could be yet attained. The romanticist, determined to defend himself with his pen alone, dismissed the urge to recruit help from the few supporters they may have earned, staring neoclassicism like a lion in the face.

The sixth and seventh stanzas could be coupled as the "Era of Uncertainty", for stanza seven also commences with a question. The image of the waves "consuming" and entombing the reflection of the moon is directed toward the idea that if romantic thought were to be swallowed by language as if it had never been given being: that would be a better "cup of ends" (or termination) than that of the irremovable scar of neoclassic plunder. Does not the lonely life of a sailor (similar to that of the romanticist in solitude and friendlessness) end in the ocean in peace? It seems only fitting that a person who spent their entire life at sea (or for the romanticist, an entire life writing) should descend into a sea-bed grave, surrounded by bright coral and crustaceans. Why could not a movement ascended from the sprout of creativity return therein unknown?

Worries and disturbing questions collect into the moon's fearful emotion of stanza eight. Becoming evident are the feelings of an individual rather than the previous maintenance of description of the romantic movement's characteristics. Yet, the image of the purple hazes' suffocating fingers creeping over the face of the lunar body, does not abandon the pattern of double meaning. Besides obstructing the moon's perception, the distorting form of haze (symbolic of fear) fogs the romanticists view of truth. The moon's expression is first addressed in this line as a "melancholic sheen". The appearance of the moon's glum face to the eyes of an earthly observer, serves as a symbol of the common romantic thinker's mental activity. He is burdened with a substantial amount of worry that he cannot overcome the threats of his enemy. Here is introduced another aspect of the war, an internal conflict; the romanticist's battle within himself. His adversary is the brevity of life, his fear that he will not be able to accomplish his goals before his earthly sojourn is finished. However, he could rejoice over the seeming immortality of his work which would outlive him (applicable to the moon's immortality).

The truth blurred by the haze is that the threats are transient and exaggerated. The moon, blinded by the mist of anxiety to the fact that he does have support, gropes in the wrong directions, and flees surreal danger. Fog has the ability to create illusions and incorrectly portray a shadowy form, which often is found to be unthreatening when the mist clears. The works of romantic poets expressed their many struggles, doubts, and anxiety, caught in the highly spiritual cloud of this mist. Thus the lines are attested: " the purple haze's threats steam grimmer (or intensify). "It's vaporizing hissings blear fate's scheme of dissipating". Inevitability lies in the evanescence of haze; it will disappear, again allowing a span of hope; and hope arrives unexpectedly.

Suddenly, the reach of the unanswered questions is broken. One small stream of light trickling through a cracked window into the prison of apprehension, clarifies the reason romanticism can never shrivel under the oppression of the oppressor. His influence has been widespread enough to summon the aid of a previously masked ally: "Earth's eyelids ope (poetical shortening of open) to needy" (or needy one, i.e. the moon).

The advent of stanza nine proposes the odd relationship between refreshment and rising tide. To marine predators the "tremor" of the water as it shifts, communicates a sense; refreshing, exciting and compelling. High tide is the time large ocean carnivores can journey farther inland seeking nourishment, without having to fear being beached. The symbolic importance of these first three lines is the comfort the romanticist draws from the sight of earth through the dissolving fog of fear. The earth (art) comprised of nature in its beauty secures a rising hope when its perfect relationship with the romantic cause is established.

William Wordsworth wrote the poem "Tintern Abbey" illustrating the comfort and encouragement he gleaned from the "deeper than physical" loveliness of nature. He viewed the natural world's presence abiding with him as a close friend's companionship.

Earth, therefore, bonds forces with the moon and initiates "drawing up a treaty", or suggesting a route of escape from bloody battle and a resolution of both the inner and outer wars the moon must face. "The terms of which might heal the blight, moon's curbing served as stemmer." Paraphrased, these two lines read; The ruin (to creativity, and the public mind of man deprived of nature's true beauty, as interpreted by the romantic; plus the certain destruction of the world, especially its oceans, robbed of influence of the lunar cycle) caused by the moons imprisonment, is possible to restore under the conditions of the statement of negotiation the moon and earth have devised.

After the words of the treaty are satisfactorily polished, a white flag is raised and waved in the sight of the enemy, who bear ready arms to crush their opposition. The word "antebellum" holds triple meaning. First, it historically portrays the time before the Civil War (the American Civil War began in 1861, romantic thought emerged at the close of the 18th century). Second and third, the flag of truce rises before a battle breaks out between the planets and the moon; or the romanticists and the neoclassicists. As before any war, negotiation is sought. At this anxious moment in time, the aura of uneasy inquiry returns. Would the romanticist's foe meet the conditions outlined in the agreement? Would the neoclassicists allow the new thought a place on the pages of literature? Should they refuse, it seemed simple for the blood of romanticism to be splattered in wadded up paper of one garbage bin. But if their desire was truly to destroy, as was apparent, no propaganda spread via newspaper, (though it might silence their opposition), would fill their hunger for utter obliteration. "Meteoric showers" depicts this relentless revenge on the celebrity of romantic thought in the language of the galaxy. "Using warfare seldom up conjured just for smooth defeat, at which a tiger cowers" This is the fear that not only will the garbage incinerator be lit and watched go up in smoke with relish, but that all ashes (remnants) left will be buried, never to be uncovered. The statement that a deemed fearless tiger would cower at the impending attack, legitimizes the moon's worries.

The timepiece drawn "pendulum of timeless ticking" is the invisible clock that has kept time throughout the ages, never to break or stop, uninfluenced by the hand of man. The control on which the world turns "that past a pleasant moment slips", no matter how precious the moment in life, time tarries for no one. Life begins, endures its short span, and retires in a continuous cycle. Note the paradox to follow: "As sunlight earth starts blocking, the clock a moment sticking". In the event of an eclipse, it appears the clock makes a move (or doesn't make) contradictory to its nature. However, this inconsistency is solely a perception. Time "freezes" only when human senses view it as doing so.

What is the eclipse? Another shadow of apprehension, its aura much more intense. This critical moment when even time seems suspended in midair, moon locked between two decisions: extension of his cause or relinquishment. While the earth cuts off the sun from the moon's view, he becomes lost (disillusioned) bemoaning the fierce darkness that destroys all beauty. He never knew the absence of light. The romanticist realizes what his journey without the sun (life) would be. He is forced to see for the first time, the aridity of art and literature without liveliness and inspiration, devoid of freedom, and grasps his cause firmer.

The romanticist meets a fork in the road. One way will terminate all endeavors he has ever undertaken. The other, a ceaseless adventure, spiced with the unknown and smeared with the possibility of abandonment and scorn. For this decision he has little time to decide whether to give up or to continue no matter what adversity is hurled his way.

The experience of enlightenment of his reason to fight for his cause by the romanticist may have occurred analogously to the following incident. The romanticist throws a snicker of ridicule on a neoclassic masterpiece he holds of symmetrically lined rows of stars in a flat sky. The picture slips from his fingers and he notices from his window the dim twilight following the sun's submergence beneath a green sea of swirling hills. The romanticist takes the initiative to lay aside his welcome bed after a hard day at work and give attention to the crisp outdoors that inspire his voice on paper. His eyes are captivated by the sparkling specks mounted on the limitless ceiling of heaven. Though he has seen them many times before, he never tires of their natural boundless wonder. Overwhelmed and inquisitive, his mind becomes like a child's. Overflowing with awe, he cannot help scorning the precise aridity of straight rows of symmetrization. There are patterns, no doubt, but all spread about in unrestrained congregations of stunning brilliance and creation. The joy of spontaneity wells up and whets the romanticist's appetite. Natural beauty is everywhere; supernatural beauty still more common. He understands his endeavor to revolutionize thought in a new, positive, firmer manner. He feels supernaturally compelled to pursue his goals with fervor no matter what walls rise against, or what strengths, what forces stand in opposition. He seizes his pencil, and rivers of emotion gush out.

Still the figure of the intercessor is ghostly as the flag of truce is carried across the battle line in attempt to strike negotiation. The mediator's seeming formlessness is due to the moons failure to believe there are forces on his side of the war. The intercessor's identity has so far gone unnoticed. This is the "bloody moment", painfully and gruesomely apprehensive. What will the enemy choose at the wave of the white flag?

All suggestions and suppositions are rent in two in a sudden, stunning shoot of light that again grabs hold of the moon. Time, in reality, uncontrolled by circumstances, could not allow the earth to any longer block the light of life. The ghostly mediator reveals himself in one dazzling, steady bolt of lightning, which does not ricochet back to its source. It sets the moon's surface aglow.

Pushed aside by the sun's fervent radiance, the dark earth is the image of language in its rigidity without life of the imagination and freedom. Not until the blinding sheer is in view, is its unsurpassed influence on the moon's world grasped. "The sun's emerging to center hold of galaxy.." Though life has existed the whole time, there was required a moment of light's concealment, that its strength might return double. The romanticist sights his advantage: life is on his side. Here, galaxy just means, in celestial terms, the shared realm of the two opposing forces, rather than the Milky Way, of which our sun is not the center.

"Whose torrid vastness glowers on radicals..." The immensity and suffocating heat of the sun glares upon the extreme enthusiast's (in support of eradicating the spontaneous and supernatural views of nature description) "...For purging the minds of spontaneity and supernatural powers." Romanticist's infatuation with powers beyond man's comprehension, and unlimited human logic to be able to meet that power, increased opposition from the left side.

The sun, which is against the planets (in life there is liberty, and liberty breaks down restraints) watches their influence dissolve as liberty overpowers. "The planets blinded, weapons vanish." A yellow sphere leaps its final step above the horizon and crawls into the jungle of darkness. The glow is welcomed in the night (romantic thought is greeted warmly by those who thirst for originality, who may be compared to the darkness tasting light. Light always overcomes darkness.)

As a convict who has spent his time in prison and is released on parole, the moon is the subject of careful vigil; but he is free! No bars to hold him in, no fear of the darkness holds legitimacy. He is "ignited" with brighter light (stronger zeal) to reach his goals.

Though many viewed "eccentric" the ideals of the romantic movement, no neoclassic rules possess authority to curb its endeavor anymore. Now "he, (romantic thought), has been invited to share with stars the ocean covers." Romantic thought is welcomed to join literature in the book of creativity alongside the contemporary poets. The moon seems to merge with earth when it appears on the water. Though it is only a reflection, the friendship and dependence on one another as symbolic counterparts cannot be undermined. The pun on covers explores the comfort mutual of human bed covers and the sea waves; a security to their environment.

"Whose once again familiar rote," the sound of lapping waves returns when the moon's gravitational management is reinstated to liven the stagnancy of the great water mass. The giant body of creativity is revived as a refreshing trickle of water delivered by an unseen hand to a lifeless form in the desert. The resuming activity of the waves "stirs shellfish in their dreaming" (resurrects imagination and beauty). This transition is a slow process by which the dead flora and fauna are replaced with flourishing life as support for their existence is reintroduced. A thought is born, and there life begins, but not until the idea is communicated (on paper or verbally) can others share in its nourishment.

The moon is described at its peak, the zenith: "between horizons hovers." In the interim of rising and setting, The moon can be at any point in the sky. It must be noted that midnight is the approximate time when the full moon reaches the meridian (imaginary line defining the center of the sky). This is also a time when the moon's glow is brightest, or the point where the most darkness comes under its influence. This is a milestone in the journey of romanticism, when its influence is at the top of literature's scale.

In the event of a full or new moon, when the sun, earth, and moon are aligned, an intriguing phenomenon involving the oceans named "spring tide" takes place. This is an interval in astronomical courses when the earth's dome of water (the bulge of ocean gravitating toward the attractions of the moon and sun) is impacted the most by the joint strength of the two magnetic celestial bodies. The result is extraordinary super-low and super-high tides, at which time, the current's effect on "sleeping shellfish" would be greatest. Increased water activity places extreme demands on all life forms within its domain, flooding the surrounding terrain. During severe low tides, normally submerged areas are exposed. One can only expect to witness dramatic effects on marine life during these surging anomalies.

Another comparison is underscored by the above paragraph of the similarities between romanticism and its lunar image in the poem. Further support is found for the drastic changes which can occur when probing imagination, inspiration, and creativity are linked. The "high tide" of romanticism has been attained.

Once again, the trek of romantic thought is likened to the voyage of a boat. The vessel spoken of in stanza fourteen, line five; however, is not in peril as it previously has been. It is "weary." But this is a positive weariness; a farmer's exhausted but triumphant glance back on a crop well harvested. The poets of this movement have slaved relentlessly, and now pause to heave a satisfied sigh. At last, the benefits of their persistent labor have become apparent when the harvest is ripe, and their reward is a place inside the covers of creativity's anthology. Again, the "ocean covers" bring security as they open up (not in a consuming way) to the romantic ideals, promising to preserve them.

An allusion to the romantic poet Wordsworth is used in line five; "A weary word's worth laden boat." The cargo this frigate carries on its transit to the next harbor is the precious knowledge that words hold the keys to the dungeons of unlettered masses and combinations to vaults brimming with the rarest gems of ingenuity. This gift grants the moon redemption from the condemnation of criticism.

William Wordsworth is most remembered for the lyrical art he produced before 1807. He expressed his trait of weariness in the uncertainty of his cause and the treasure of the romantic endeavor. Later in life's journey it is not clear whether the attacks of doubt, the mutiny of a close friend and writing companion, or dissatisfaction and loss of vigor stemming from the departure and failure of dear and loved channels of inspiration (the French revolution, family loss) played a larger role in the poet's disenchantment. The sad result was his "jumping of ship" to team irreversibly with conventionalism.

But this incident did not result in much weakening of the movement. If anything it broadened, arranged its dispersal, and was implanted in young hearts. Wordsworth's commemoration will remain in his production of the original attitude toward nature, the values of which he brought to life, preserving the worth of the written word.

The redemptive values of romantic thought are shared with the human characteristics of the moon's face; "assumed identity of mortal." The moon's eyes are described first, portrayed as being attracted by "simple land." Simplicity is yet another essential component; an additional strand in the web of romanticism. The movement creates its own world where two things deemed incompatible can coexist. Simple things can be drawn out of the ocean of complexity and vice versa. Just like parents often use simple, understandable language and examples to explain something confusing to their child, so the romanticist skillfully utilizes words.

Earth and moon are very different. One appears naked of any life form, while the other is teeming with flora and fauna of all life forms. One is cold, ashen, and, as many would admit, gloomy, but its opposite is bright, green, and bubbling. One is crusty and dry, while the other flows with streams of an immeasurable and unharnessable substance called water.

The most enchanting happenstance is when the surfaces of these two spheres meet. Glued to the top of that water substance of earth is the moon's brazen body on a cloudless night. The two converge, both shapes, both round, and both sharing the solar system. No human or any effort in the universe can separate the duo in this intimate moment. Though one can hold the other tenderly, the limbless other can only fondle with eyes at a distance.

Lips make the man in the moon's face complete. They are "round in thought" and "grow wider." The literal moon appears to have searching eyes and an open mouth of shock and sorrow. But the symbolic reflection is more significant here. The quality of roundness shouts forth "fully developed" on the streets anxiously awaiting news. Mature thought retraces its steps to the romantic view that effective poetry cannot be produced without ample meditation on a given subject. An idea or experience causing an emotion or response which stimulates the poet to put his pencil to use, is therefore delayed in his mental engine until it collects enough vigor (grows wider) in order for him to replicate the feeling cleverly on paper. The idea or encounter that results from this deep contemplation is the "new life at mental portal."

The moon has neither a hand nor fingers to hold a writing utensil bursting with potential creation, ("verse-filled pencil") but the poet does. The pencil is the channel that transports ideas from the mind, transforms them into words, and imprints them on a page. After careful meditation, the romanticist is ready to utilize his vehicle of communication, which allows him to share his discoveries and encounters concisely with his fellow man.

One who speaks of that which he is familiar; that which he has observed, felt, or studied about, is an "experience reciter." Often, since the theme of romantic poetry was usually the writer's feelings about certain events, wants, hopes, or problems, it was founded on experience.

Only two allusions occur in the entire poem, and are made of a pair of highly influential romantic pioneers: William Wordsworth and Samuel Taylor Coleridge. Coauthors of Lyrical Ballads, both men had much influence on the romantic movement, and for a time, enjoyed fruitful companionship. Sadly, the strong tie between them was to be traumatically severed by disagreement, a scar which would be never fully removed.

If these two men represented the heavenly bodies spoken of in the poem, Coleridge would be the moon, for his many works acquainted with the supernatural, magical, and mysterious. Whereas, Wordsworth could be none other than the earth, companion of nature, in thought, profound as the wind over a purling brook. The dual picture agrees with the friendship of the moon and earth, disjoined, yet connected, and the paradoxical leaning of romanticism itself. The allusion in the first line of stanza sixteen, refers to the lunar character as much as to the romanticist. At any time the moon is not wholly lit, it has a "cooler" or colder and darker "edge" or part than the section reflecting the sun's light to earth (not to mention the always present "dark side" of the moon since it is a sphere, and like the earth, cannot be covered by the sun's light all at one time; part of its surface will be turned away). When the moon is not full, (to human perception) only earthshine (the effect of the sun's light being reflected off the earth's oceans, creating an indistinct visibility of the darkened portion of the moon; only at night) can reveal that the lunar body is still a sphere. This phenomenon demonstrates the mysterious act of the moon only appearing to change shape. This illusion is regulated by the moon's monthly cycle, as well as by the positions of the orbs. Similarly, mystery is what Coleridge seasoned his writings with, from which inspiration could be gleaned by those who shared his passion. The legacy of romanticism will not die with the "browning page of history," thanks to the work of those who saw value in originality, freedom, imagination and creativity. The new outlook grants its name and gift to all who wish to join the movement. Again like a vessel with a new, young captain, the moon embarks once more on a route of ceaseless adventure. The library of ideas and insight stacked in the intellect is as vast as the sky, as numerous as the stars that compose it. Each new thought communicated, stimulates a novel voyage, and the sea of creation expands. Every mind bears the capacity to produce art.

The literal moon traverses the sky, and though its "tracks" are invisible, it never deviates from his cycle; and the pattern, when observed closely, becomes apparent. Its journey follows the same arch across the celestial heights it did on its maiden voyage. Romanticism is also in a way in constant motion; improving, growing and dispersing.

If the moon were romanticism, he would speak. Though his voice would be inaudible, it would be clear to the seeker of freedom that he'd encourage "Think, think on the real and the right. Don't, don't let discouragement blight. Lift, lift up your pencil and write. Go, train your utensil and fight." To the cultivator of imagination and creativity he'd call "Look! Novel ideas sail not far off; determination will carry you there." To the lover of nature he would proclaim "examine the minuscule, watch the unobserved, then the larger things not sensed by those who have only considered the enormous, will be understood by you. Have patience and vigilance, and shame those whose impatience has dragged them under the drowning surface of conventionalism. To leaders, the moon's words would ring "Stand on the rock and probe the sea, holding your beacon high, find vessels lost before they be beached on the shore nearby. Stand in your place and humble be. Don't let a sailor die. When you're a guide who'll others see, all will respect your eye. But above all this, there is a tone of urgency in the moon's voice. "Behold" in caution he orates "what the highly praised romantic thought bypassed, what the romanticist did not discern, what the poet overlooked in all his acclaimed wisdom. He saw nature, it dazzled in his eyes, and he idolized creation. The companionship he thought he found in nature was as fleeting as his days, numbered, nearing their limit. His searching soul dissatisfied, he tried to alienate himself from humanity, when sin's effects became real to him. But he did not grip the truth and refused to acknowledge his own lost state. Recognizing his mortality and inability to escape mankind's ills, (for he, in fact, was human) he summoned the help of the supernatural, hoping to find comfort. Yet he still relived his first mistake: he refused to acknowledge the Almighty Creator, who, in all His majesty, had wrought the romanticist's world, and could provide the answers to all his doubts, needs, and worries. "Be wise; listen to the proclamation of creation, rather than the distorted view of man. Created things shout from the fields, in the sky, and from the depths, that an infinitely wise, loving Hand crafted all these, beneath the influence of which all things tremble in holy reverence and awe. The creatures know a perfect Maker, who breathes stars and leaves a thundering cloud of fire in His wake. Nature, which is part of the Heavenly Father's creation, has no power to give life, bless, or kill. It is the Omniscient, Omnipotent, God who perfectly controls all. No thing begins without His initiation. All creation begins in His mind. All forces draw their influence from the Giver.

Perhaps the next clear night you view the astral twinklings in the sky, the bright moon, or the fierce sunlight by day, you will observe with new wonder the Poet and His poetry, that lacks no beat, has a unique and perfect rhythm, and an unjustified, constant mood of love.

ABOUT THE AUTHOR

Anna Davis was born in September of 1998. She grew up on the evergreen blanketed northwest coast of Oregon, where one has to find entertaining things to do during the all year round rainy season.   At twelve, Anna began writing poetry. Her favorite subject being language arts, Anna's love of poetry grew as she discovered a simple, fun, and artistic way to put words together. Friends started reading and enjoying her poetry. She was given lessons by a family friend on the mechanics of poetry. The beautiful world of poetry opened up before her, and her adventures into it added up. At the age of eighteen, Anna had enough material to put a book together; which became this, her first book to be published.

Made in the USA
San Bernardino, CA
17 January 2019